CW01082087

Re·creation /// edited by Éadaoín Lynch & Alycia Pirmohamed

Re·creation

A Queer Poetry Anthology

edited by Éadaoín Lynch
& Alycia Pirmohamed

– Stewed Rhubarb Press –

Published in 2022 by
Stewed Rhubarb Press
Tarland, Aberdeenshire

www.stewedrhubarb.org

ISBN: 978-1-910416-23-5

Copyright remains with the respective poets

Cover art: 'An Octagonal Mirror' by Benny Nemer

Thanks to Creative Scotland for their generous
support towards the publication of this book.

'Josephine Baker Finds Herself' by Patience Agbabi previously
appeared in Bloodshot Monochrome (Canongate, 2008)
'La Hora de las Brujas / Shamaness' by Antonela Pallini-Zemin
was previously published in Harana Poetry, Issue 6.

Printed by Imprint Digital, UK

*Stewed Rhubarb Press are Charlie Roy and Duncan Lockerbie. We and
Re·creation editors Éadaoín Lynch and Alycia Pirmohamed would like to
thank Benny Nemer for permission to reproduce 'An Octagonal Mirror' as our
cover image, Gillebrìde Mac 'IlleMhaoil for his Gaelic proofreading, Gutter
Magazine, Scottish BPOC Writers Network and Lighthouse for supporting
the application to Creative Scotland, Vahni Anthony Ezekiel Capildeo for
contributing the foreword, Eddie Gibbons for his proofreading, and Beth
Cochrane for her editorial expertise.*

Contents

elegy for callie gardner · **Nat Raha** · VIII

Foreword · **Vahni Anthony Ezekiel Capildeo** · XI

Introduction · **Éadaoín Lynch & Alycia Pirmohamed** · XIII

* * *

Leave Tae Live · **Kira Scott** · 1

Chrysanthemum 菊 · **Jinhao Xie** · 2

Now · **Oluwaseun Olayiwola** · 4

Yarrow · **Jack Cooper** · 5

Carcinisation as Coping Mechanism · **Sam J Grudgings** · 6

Glance · **Mary Jean Chan** · 7

Josephine Baker Finds Herself · **Patience Agbabi** · 8

El Diablo · **Mariam Varsimashvili** · 10

Pierced · **Mina C** · 12

Gay Jesus · **Mae Diansangu** · 14

First Touch · **Kat Payne Ware** · 16

Behind This Mask / Another Mask · **JP Seabright** · 17

Tenement · **Dean Atta** · 20

domestic: portrait · **Andrew McMillan** · 21

I Cannot Weave (A Conversation) · **Lady Red Ego** · 22

air ii · **Christopher Kirubi/Dove** · 24

La Hora de las Brujas / Shamaness
    Antonela Pallini-Zemin · 27

An Ordered List of Barriers to Queer Intimacy [extracts]
    jack/lilidh · 29

Cearcall-Suidhe / Toilet Seat
    Christopher Whyte · 34–35

Eulogy for a Young Sailor · **Jay Gao** · 36

The River Turns into a Waterfall · **Andrés N. Ordorica** · 38

Under God's Eye · **Courtney Conrad** · 40

Museum of Survival; exhibit s.1516891
  Helen Bowie · 41

ghazal: a sign from Allah · **Deenah Al-Aqsa** · 42

the Long Mynd · **Jack Bigglestone** · 44

Norway · **Kat Dixon** · 45

Mellishon · **Harry Josephine Giles** · 46

everyone is still alive. · **Joelle Taylor** · 47

* * *

About the Poets · 53

elegy for callie gardner   /// *Nat Raha*

ok, so if the natural sciences
                                     skewed
        on the installation of their world

                        ,

                        our gravities exert like
                        the moon in relation , legs

                exquisite to this north
                  grove is a groove on enjambment ,
                        the music we pull/ed from the dictionary
                        paper knitting lines into friends, flutter
                                        over wrought-gates
                                        ,, we make
                kin w/ diasporic arbours
                quiet calling your poems
                                        , let their
                intimations vibrate, seep sonics into cones

                        ꞏꞏ but the(ir) garden calls time, en-
                                closing around us, non
                -natives whisked from ground
                                the logic of conservation
                                after the asphyxiation of the earth

        – that's how all the conversations go now. let's
        meet on our bikes, worn hearts, speed off isolation
                                as bells usher,

heron lands high, young, looksout
      knows the depth of the basin where
      i home among eiders – no, lock us in
with
  our fauna, anxiety, poems
     , the heterosexuals tying themselves up

    & even
   in their endless day, still
     harmonics beautiful gorging
& then the ground aflame, grouse felled
by the gun, in the
     nowhere we sow flowers unbeknownst

bereft of conversation in
    grievous summer, gossip of the south
-side, the state of the soil & libraries

    & half of the moon still spinning

eyes attend brightest nights in bloom—
we forget our work for a few hours, move to life
among the worms, the birds—

eighteenth august, 2021

Foreword

That the anthology *Re·creation* begins with Nat Raha's elegy and ends with Joelle Taylor's *everyone is still alive.* is no accident. Here are journeys of queer joy: not straight, from hidden to open or singular to plural or grief to gladness, but circling, cycling, dipping, licking, napping, dancing. Recreation, without the middle dot – without the break – is a leisure trap of the governing orders' tyrannous fictions of the 'natural'. Such 'recreation' is 'R&R', rest and recreation, rest and recuperation between school disciplines or corporate missions. Giving that recreation a break, *re·creation* – this world of words recovers the ancient sense of creating anew.

Reading this anthology as a kind of Eden – where there is no gender; where binary conformity is the perverse result of some kind of easy-money fall; where the spirit of creation is always plural, in loving communion with itself, whispering beauty in the tiniest detail while brooding on the vast – so we are re-turned, perfectly creaturely, to a time beyond dead-naming, a time of messages that surpass market-driven rhetoric of unitary self or documents of hurt imposed by society's un/natural order.

Nuance lives, in breath, thinking-with, hesitation, palimpsest; in poems of thoughtful typography. These push up against the margin; allow themselves pauses and overruns; refuse to reduce the complexity of the human interface with the page, making marks as if, as and when, because, just because.

These forms amount to celebration, renewing the possibilities of how we inhabit language in print, a shareable way of inhabiting each other's lovely strangeness. Scrolling through, I note at random some authors who transfigure the face of the page: Kat Payne Ware, Jack Bigglestone, Dove Maina, Josie Giles. By virtue of the anthology format, every form tendrils towards, resonates with, and co-illumines every other; a gathering, in truth.

I am struck by how gently these poets dissolve boundaries between the 'self' and 'other', 'past' and 'present'. Long gone are the old poetics whereby a mountain must be conquered, or rainfall represent human melancholy, or a landscape be likened to a gendered body. Kira Scott holds hands with the late Nan Shepherd, who pulls her into the palm of the Cairngorms. Antonela Pallini-Zemin sings 'a world of abrazos, de lazos de amor'. Dean Atta charts lovers from verbal strife to Sunday cleaning in reconciliatory silence.

This earth is laced with love; we, and the dust, part of the imaginative, gentle housework.

Vahni Anthony Ezekiel Capildeo, 2022

Introduction

For this anthology, based in Scotland and looking out to the UK and the rest of the world, it is only fitting to open with Nat Raha's heartfelt tribute to Callie Gardner. Callie's passing on 8th July 2021 was a shock to the literary and queer communities, and it had been our early intention as editors to invite Callie to participate in the anthology.

One of Callie's last poems, 'fifth letter / moonletter,' writes about how 'we go out roaming with a hangry heart.' We hope the work you read here inspires you to be just as hangry, as forceful, and as kind as them.

Ways and Means

Re·creation borrows its title from a poem by the incomparable Audre Lorde, a self-described Black, lesbian, mother, warrior, poet. In her poem, the act of creativity is understood as pleasure, and pleasure itself an act of creativity. We chose this word not only for its commitment to Lorde, and the intersectional feminism she stood for, but also these ideas of play, refreshment, recovery, restoration, and invigoration.

With Scotland-based independent publisher Stewed Rhubarb Press, Re·creation invited queer creatives to write poems, develop their craft, build a community, and be published in a landmark poetry anthology. One of our aims was to respond to the Covid-19 pandemic, emphasising professional opportunities and networking during a time of isolation and financial distress for many. The anthology includes 29 poets – 9 solicited poets, 20 selected from an open submission call. Final selections for the book were chosen by a team of seven altogether: the two co-editors, two guest readers, and three members of Stewed Rhubarb Press. From the open call, we received over 270 submissions (nearly 900 poems) and recruited our two guest readers to help select our final poems for the anthology.

Workshops, round-table feedback, and 1-to-1 mentorship were also part of the project, free to the attendees, and all contributors received a £100 fee for their published piece. Our development opportunities were intended to provide support to underrepresented groups and were all held online. Re·creation was built and run as a community building experience, one that allowed the contributors to continue pursuing creative goals after the project was completed.

Transparency and accessibility have been priorities from the outset and we were keen to build them into the process. For any poets who were not accepted from the open call, we offered editorial feedback, and provided it to over 70 respondents. To select work from the open call, we recruited two BIPOC guest readers to ensure fairness across our shortlisting. As part of our values of equality and accessibility, we ensured there would be no submission fee to offer work in the open call, and no requisite or expectation of prior publication experience. We set up a simple webform for the open call, and no cover letter, supporting statement, or CV were required. We also made some places available in our workshops for contributors from our longlist who had not been selected for the anthology.

We couldn't achieve any of the aims of the project as a team of two alone. Our application to Creative Scotland was supported by letters from Stewed Rhubarb Press, the Scottish BPOC Writers Network, Gutter Magazine, and Lighthouse Bookshop. We are forever indebted to them. A small network of people simply willing to bet on an idea was all that made Re·creation happen, and it's our sincerest hope that Re·creation has offered the same confidence and care for the poets within these pages and outside them.

Representing Poetry

As we were preparing for this project, foremost in our minds was the ongoing barriers to success for those in the margins: writers of colour, writers with disabilities, women writers, writers with caring responsibilities, older writers, and those of religious minorities. According to a report from 2020, commissioned by the Scottish BPOC Writers Network, the lack of successful writers with a similar background to their own was 'a particular challenge to 51% of BAME writers' (as opposed to 21% of white writers). Additionally, as cited by the Royal Society of Literature in 2019, the most commonly cited challenges to a writer's early life are the combined lack of financial income, time, and confidence.

Recommendations from these and other reports

include: recognising structural inequalities, offering development opportunities to writers early in their career, understanding that no one demographic is homogenous, taking responsibility to address inequalities in the literary sector, and challenging views that suggest diversity and quality are incompatible. As we were fashioning the structure of this project, we took these recommendations to heart and aimed to prioritise equalities, diversity and inclusion along the intersections of our poets.

Our central focus – the development of queer voices and delivery of an anthology platforming their work – has always been fundamentally intersectional. As a project funded by Creative Scotland and based in Edinburgh, we are also delighted that it features poems in Scots and Gaelic. We are particularly proud that over half of this anthology is from BIPOC poets, that over a third is from trans* and genderqueer poets, and that we have poets of every adult age group.

There is always more to do to uplift and support anyone living in the margins. Re·creation was one small enterprise to that aim, running as a sustainable, ethical, replicable process. We hope that our measurable successes inspire and prompt others in the sector to pursue projects like this and continue to promote and encourage writers of all minorities.

The Anthology

Every anthology, whether attempting to encapsulate a snapshot or a comprehensive overview, will fail – and the failure is necessary. Neither attempt is attainable or, frankly, desirable. By nature of being a queer anthology, any parameters we set on subject or context are inherently porous and undercut. This means there will inevitably be gaps, lacunae, and absences in this book.

Though we are proud and thrilled to have such strong representation from BIPOC poets, trans* and genderqueer poets, and every adult age group, there should be more representation from poets over 45, poets based outside Scotland and the UK, poets writing in languages other than English, and poets with disabilities. Anthologies, ours included, are limited by constraints of book length, budget, page size, and time, in addition to issues of consistency and diversity. We sincerely hope our failures here will galvanise others to try and succeed. When we look back on this book in years to come, we will no doubt notice more absences and failures we don't see now – and that shift in perspective is essential and right.

In our original aims, as well as our submission call, we claimed that we sought 'personal poetry,' written out of first-hand experience. Mostly, this claim was born out of the desire to centre queer voices, but not narrow into a niche theme. (We also couldn't decide on just one theme anyway.) We were starting something new, during a Covid lockdown, and had several learning curves ahead of us. Trans poets in our community rightfully corrected us on the problem of asking for personal poetry, noting that their bodies are 'already politically overdetermined,' that their authenticity 'relentlessly commoditised,' and their visibility is 'both trap and door.' Our appreciation for such honesty can't be overstated; because of this feedback, we amended the call to invite submissions that directly challenge visibility and commodification. We know that this expansion has made the anthology a better book, and Re·creation a better project.

Return

We encourage you to dip in and out of this book as you like. You'll find unpredictable shifts in theme, style, form, and subject. You'll find work that surprises you, that confronts you, and work that intrigues you. Some of the best experiences of reading are ahead of you: what you feel days or weeks afterwards. Moments when you're undertaking a mundane task and a line comes back to you out of the blue and fills you up from your soles, or you notice something new that you remember reading about, knowing you wouldn't have noticed it otherwise. Poetry is not often perceived as a democratic form, but in the house of Re·creation, we hope there is a poem for everyone. We wish you might find it in these pages.

When this book is published, it will join a range of queer poetry books that did not exist when *Re·creation* was first dreamed up. In 2021, Anamot Press published their poetry anthology *The Sun Isn't Out Long Enough,* a book that transcends national borders and showcases queer experiences told without shame. 2021 saw at least three more collections of queer work, including Lifeboat Press, which published *Queering the Green*, an unprecedented collection of Irish queer poetry; Muswell Press, which published *Queer Life, Queer Love,* a collection of fiction, non-fiction, and poetry; and Arkbound, which published the *Writing Our Space: An LGBTQ+ Anthology of essays, short stories and poems.* In 2022, Vintage launched their anthology *100 Queer Poems,* edited by our very own contributors Mary Jean Chan and Andrew McMillan, another book that transcends borders, and also time, as it celebrates both contemporary voices and visionary poets of the past. May there be many, many more.

Return to this book as often as you want & know you are always welcome. And in the words of one of our cherished guest readers, Harvey Dimond:

> It was an honour to have this experience and to be able to read such a breadth and diversity of writing, much of which touched on issues and experiences that are close to my heart.

> There are so many talented poets in the following pages, and I hope you enjoy reading their work as much as I did.

Éadaoín Lynch and Alycia Pirmohamed
Edinburgh, 2022

Leave Tae Live   /// *Kira Scott*

An ode tae Nan Shepherd

I hud awready climbed many mountains
before I bagged ma first munro.

The lines eh her words ran like paths eh a map,
a pull intae the palm eh the Cairngorms;
guidin me through the deepest glens
and beckonin me across the highest ridges.

She hud held ma hand as the other spread wide
tae encompass the view fi Ben Macdui's summit.
We swam in the depthless pits eh Loch A'on,
and afterwards lay oan oor backs tae watch the gauzy clouds –

all long before I hud experienced the unfettered
delight eh standing in the drifting sky;
the peaty land below looking jist as miniscule
as it does fi a plane windae.

Chrysanthemum 菊   /// *Jinhao Xie*

I lost my virginity
in a bathtub
to my brother's electric toothbrush. Ha ha.
But, that didn't count.
It was chrysanthemum season then. I lost
something. The barren window and sky
was grey as a sparrow's belly.
It was around 3 pm. Saturday.
Mum was still at work.
No one was home so I got naked
in her bathroom. The television was on
full volume, showing my favourite cartoons.
In front of a steamed mirror, I stood
for a long, long time.
My face softened by the damp dust,
I couldn't recognise
if I was a girl, with undeveloped breasts; or
if I was a 'boy'.
The chrysanthemum gel ejected. Empty bottle.
Water gushed out of faucet like crystal
tadpoles. Spume into tiny islands. I saw
a seraphic self dipped in paradise.
No shame, not yet.
Curiosity tickled my chrysanthemum cheeks
I could feel my body surrendering to physics.
Afloat.

Before, I had only seen chrysanthemums
in late Springs.
Never thought that my body could be
a host of such beauty. Never knew
such possibility burying in me. Never felt so soft
and of this earthly ocean. I withheld
my breath, under water. Let the verdurous roots
take their ground on me. Like magic, bubbles
quaked on the surface, my eyes shut and I
let my chrysanthemum bloom to its fullest.

Now   /// *Oluwaseun Olayiwola*

suppose the body.
suppose the body is a city.
suppose the body is a city the way love, as if
we could ruin it, naively, seems
a river—suppose we are in that river, its dark
orders come-and-gone like words, the skin's
weighted cage a name that needs
forgottenness—forgottenness—
what we can't escape, samsara
to which we are bound, circles
of our drowned mouths vacating
the light, releasing a sound our ears
do not hear, waves
extinguished, an embrace, a nothingness—

*

Then we're on the shore again.
The stars, from this angle, wet and shining.

Hiss of the wind stirring above us
in a music, in a moan—

He slides his hand into my city

and in my city
his hand
is disappeared

Yarrow   /// *Jack Cooper*

*"Yarrow became associated with testing a lover's faithfulness: the
herb was pushed up the lover's nose and rotated several times – if
the lover was faithful, the enquirer's nose would bleed."*
  – *Caz Hildebrand, Herbarium (2016)*

I come to the alder at dusk,
undergrowth stopping six palms from its trunk
            a ragged fairy ring
and find him waiting again.

I kneel,
let him feed a faggot of yarrow to my throat
and twist,
florets tearing loose on my tongue,
roots thick with the scent of selfish, unworked soil,
birdsong a pulsating tinnitus,
my lover relentless until
            we fall from each other
not waiting to see who bleeds first.

Carcinisation as Coping Mechanism   /// *Sam J Grudgings*

I become   a crab   again.
The taxonomy   of shy   discovery.

Adapted   to the crushing   depth
how the lack   of light   has a weight.

Find a shell   big enough   to fit all my promises
my actions   have   consequences, I am sure

the line   of inheritors   behind me
will find   this protection   fit for purpose.

Bottom feeder, cadaver eater, sift particle
message receiver. Swear this intervention is temporary,
empty the exoskeleton pocket of a day.
Hera-sent hermit, living bottled ships. Mostly

sideways dancer,   potted delicacy,   volcanic vent
noxious fume breather,   crunched wet   endless phantom

church skinned   sacculina eunuch,   orphanage bodied
toxic-lunged, carcass   -architect, ribcage   rattler

I'm content to have   adapted to a   ubiquitous form
a shadows   patience gifted   with statute

we'll reinvent   a fresh narrative
ourselves   kinder gods
we all long for,   all deserve

intricately planned pincer formation
you will become, eventually. Ouroboros of gracious anatomy.
most fervent revolution. If I get anywhere close to out of here,
promise not to drag me back

Glance   /// *Mary Jean Chan*

Today, the fear of drag festers. You are four, five, six, seven, eight, nine, ten and refusing to wear a dress again. How a body endures the toll of another's glance. In the apartment, speech unravels like smoke. Outside, the moon is losing her mind. Mother and Child now divided. Her smile was once a gate you unbolted. Wind came through like fate. She told you that a mother's love is the one unsinkable ship. You remember this as you wander into the forsaken hours between reckoning and breakfast.

Josephine Baker Finds Herself
/// *Patience Agbabi*

She picked me up
like a slow-burning fuse. I was down
that girls' club used to run in Brixton,
on acid for fuel. Lipstick lesbians,
techno so hardcore it's spewing out Audis.
She samples my heartbeat and mixes it with
vodka on the rocks. I'm her light-skinned, negative,
twenty-something, short black wavy-bobbed diva.
She purrs *La Garçonne, fancy a drink?* I say
Yes. She's crossing the Star Bar like it's a catwalk. So sleek!
A string of pearls, her flapper dress
studded with low-cut diamonds
through my skin, straight to my heart.
Twenties chic! She works
me up and down. I worship
the way she looks.

The way she looks
me up and down. I worship
twenties chic. She works
through my skin, straight to my heart
studded with low-cut diamonds.
A string of pearls her flapper dress.
Yes! She's crossing the Star Bar like it's a catwalk so sleek
she purrs, la garçonne! *Fancy a drink?* I say.
Twenty-something, short, Black, wavy-bobbed diva:
Vodka on the rocks, I'm her light-skinned negative.
She samples my heartbeat and mixes it with
techno so hardcore it's spewing out Audis
on acid for fuel. *Lipstick Lesbians,*
that girls' club used to run in Brixton
like a slow-burning fuse. I was down.
She picked me up.

El Diablo /// *Mariam Varsimashvili*

He is a belly
full of cherry pits,
part man,
part memory.

Desire backwards,
a journey to school,
the ruins of an old
bathing pool where
women

slashed each other with
compliments.

and didn't emerge for
days. I licked morello
jam off the pink tiles.

We made love on a rooftop
saturated with sunshine, his
body a thorn that pierced
religious symbols:

a curved shell,
an impaled pomegranate,
a cloud in the shape of an
elephant's trunk.

on a ripple of linen.

I was keeping watch on a
steeple when I bled
yellow paint.

Handled everything with
gloves from then on.
Bleached my hair, painted
streaks of blue on the
ceiling.

I know he is mine:
I painted a mural on the
back of his throat so I
wouldn't forget.

A trail of saliva leaks down
his spine, Latin etched into
his bones.

I've been inside him.
I crawled into his guts

The house we lived in was a
rotten tooth.

It came alive when
he touched me, dreaming
with one wooden foot
in the afterlife,

while the other, soft
marrow of a fawn's
leg, stood

When we kissed for too
long, I saw stars – my
body ascending for a
while, tracing scars.

In the garden, there is a
statue of him as he was
and will forever be:

white oleander night
flames, staying in bed all
day, eating peach compote
out of a small
jar.

Pierced /// *Mina C*

twelve years earlier / ma and her mother-in-law hunched over / a photo album assembled by another grandmother / overseas / pointing at the rings orbiting your earlobes / behind the cot slats / they take turns to insist buying real silver / in southall / was worth it / you roll your eyes / stare down at your right arm / wonder if a steel bangle could crack bottle tops open / steel like / cutlery in the canteen at school / steel like / the smell of glasses of milk / poured into potted plants / steel like the 207 / exhaust fumes curling around your legs / later / in the back of some piercing shop / flanked by fresh produce / you shift / thigh to thigh / waiting / for a woman whose face is studded like a galaxy / 'this won't hurt for long' / she says / 'just a little pinch / deep breaths / now' she says / everyone comes back with piercings in september / you think / the needle punctures through / you swear you invent the sound / of the cartilage cracking / heat of it filling your nose / like milk / filling a baby's body when it feeds / for the first time / 'barely a pinch' the woman said / stepping back / everyone comes back / with matching studs / you tell myself that souls were twinned / genderless / like pairs of earrings / like couplets / daughter twinned with another / gold studs / two daughters / two garlands / too little / too much / you ask a woman to cut your hair off / in the bathroom / the nose stud pops out / won't go back in / you faint on the floor / of the hairdresser's / and learn that / when your body disappears / it is your hair that leaves first / so you keep it cut short / start punctuating your poems /

with needles / and start sleeping with two / or three / pairs
of earrings / something tiny to weigh you down / in case you
evaporate / again / in the album / you are a baby again / on
ma's bed / towelled with a gold chain / around the neck / a
pendant that tastes like / home in your mouth / at night / last
week you let someone kiss you / with tongue / afterwards you
swear / you feel the chain loosen itself / around your neck /
you find the pendant burning / a hole into your bra / the next
morning you wake up / with a sore throat / the shame of it /
like a lozenge / in your mouth

Gay Jesus   /// *Mae Diansangu*

gay jesus

turns	water into buckfast
sucks	the fever from a young boy's blood and
swallows	
serves	
feeds	the children
offers	his flesh on a plate so the hungry can
	taste him enter him and live there
queers	the law of nature
sashays	across water
knows	the sanctity of bodily fluids
converts	saliva into salvation
spits	to switch on blind eyes
laughs	when mary [the bestie from bethany]
	tickles his feet with her hair
gets high	off this sacred rebellion: intimacy between
	two reviled bodies
is	a pisces sun aquarius moon scorpio rising
has	daddy issues
kisses	judas back
whispers	*i have waited my whole life for this*
knows	he was purpose built to be kissed by this man

gladly follows   god's plan along the edge of his tongue
bleeds   honest wounds that tease the soldier who
   wants to fuck him, but kills him instead
dies   afraid and unashamed the patron saint
   of those brutalised by the state
dies   in vain his mother at his feet
weeps   to know his sacrifice means nothing
   when his siblings on earth are crucified

First Touch /// *Kat Payne Ware*

as a form of breaking:locally disturbed by the resulting shock:breaking:an implication of permanence:licking and/or touching and/or breathing into another mouth:a bodily exchange:a pulling noise:the breaking away of a part from a whole:the first touch of a body to another body/of water:shores as holding space:the shore as a form of uncertainty:un/sure:and the breaking of a wave:breaking and regathering itself in/to something massive and un/holdable:if bodies are held they are held by other bodies:leakage happens:it is impossible to contain some/thing entirely:it will find the breakage and drop through it like an egg:solidity in falling and waves lapping and spreading:the gelatinous rolling of forms from one containment to another even a spider within a room is contained by the room:the sea is contained within its designated premises:only a lapping:as if premonition were a forward/backward movement:just as a lake sitting under a sky becomes the sky:tapestried lakes and mountains are as real as lakes and mountains:one does not contain the other:they contain themselves via a breakage from meaning:continents drift along like benign meringues:the water carries them and reconvenes around them a demonstration of permission:as a licking which re/winds itself and licks again:wetness reconvening with the air and falling:through breakage with its own suspended form:touching the ground explosively as kissing:as breaking something

Behind This Mask / Another Mask
/// *JP Seabright*

PARIS, 1920-1937

Too extreme for surrealists
too real
you walked it / wore it / shaved it / braved it all
while Breton was playing parlour games
Your own authentic self
with bound breasts and painted lips
a mask / of a masque / of a masc-identity
intentionally neutered
but never neutral
Dali did not know what to do with you

The flagrancy of degenerate art
gender agenda alter ego
anti-erotic trompe l'oeil
Your life a performance / mise-en-scène
your lover as audience / creator / muse / camera
co-performer / co-llaborator
All is equal in love and war

Cancelled Confessions / Don't Kiss Me
"I will never finish removing
all these masks"
You queered the circle /
so ahead of yourself
we've still not caught up

JERSEY, 1937-1945

Self-Portrait of The Artist As a Radical Act
of Resistance
mocking their goosestepped parade
photomontage as anti-propaganda
Fortune teller / teller of truth / with your paper
bullets / homemade bricolage
detonating in Nazi pockets
the soldier without a name
and still your name / still now
subverted / unknown

Ten months in an Occupied Jersey Jail
solitary / always solitary / always together
your lover / step-sister / partner in crimes
against the War / *ohne Ende*
Geschlechtkrieg - the succoured bite
of that German Eagle
a bit between your teeth

Signal / Mirror / Soldier Manoeuvres
Your ambiguity confuses them
on autoportrait not autopilot
"Until I see everything clearly /
I want to hunt myself down /
struggle with myself"

JERSEY, 2005

Buried in St Brelade cemetery
            buried / forgotten / your queerness
straightened out / confessions cancelled
        masks misunderstood / gender denied
the hand holding the mirror /
        looking at us / looking away
the invisible adventure
        made invisible again
fifty years after your death
        they still don't know what to do with you

Sans Nom / retrospective exhibition
        museum masquerade / disguising you both
referencing ~~always~~ only as step-sisters
        not as lovers / lesbians / queer / partners / The Third
Sex / life-long loving companions
        co-creators / co-conspirators
in your transgressive arts

Claude & Suzanne / Lucy & Marcel
        Bending gender / until it breaks
until it means nothing / until it
        "no longer resembled human form"
Retro-heterosexualised / the one mask
            you did not choose to wear

/// Dedicated to Claude Cahun & Marcel Moore ///

Tenement /// *Dean Atta*

I don't know if I want to be here
in our two bedroom tenement flat in Battlefield
or in the listed building on Queen's Park Drive
you take me to view.

'If it's warmth you're after, a tenement might not
be for you,' says one half of the gay couple
showing us around their home of six years,
as if I don't know the cold of tenement living.

'We've decided it's time to upgrade
to a house,' the other half tells us, as if looking down
the property and relationship ladder.
After the viewing, we slip into a two-day argument.

Then, it's Sunday: we clean as we do each week,
radio playing, no need to speak. I wonder
how to clean the radiator gaps, grimacing teeth of heat,
gathering dust for the two years we've lived here.

I purchase a cleaning tool that boasts
removing dust will reduce the risk of fire.
I'd never thought of dust, fragments of us
and our living, at risk of catching alight.

I'll wait, again, for Sunday
to dislodge dust, doubt and fear,
along with cruel words we've spoken here
accumulating in hard to reach places.

domestic: portrait   /// *Andrew McMillan*

we've been here before you and I   this bed
and outside the untuned radio of rain
against the window   and the birds speaking
through it into the high dusk of summer

before the breaking   the sky was that shade
of pink when the peony has blown its petals
and left its jesters hat hanging on the stem
now it's the long black chimney of the goose's neck

relentless   and the toungehiss of water
on the path   tomorrow will be clearing
the hedgerow of its upturned mantelpiece
of bric-a-brac brought in by the storm

but for now we have this easy frequency
of side by side   this bed we propped with books
last night to hold off imminent collapse
we've been there before   you and I

I Cannot Weave (A Conversation)
/// *Lady Red Ego*

SAPPHO:

The magic came again.
It visited my fingertips.
Bed-death, la petite.
The female prefix, a default
for other women to lay
beneath. I have lied.
I have waited. You are not a man,
too refined, the soft jut of your chin,
the narrow bone of your hip. I have
told them other names you go by,
titles like violet and mister and
Achilles. Sir, there is no need
to obscure your body. His breast
fills my mouth like a wine cup about to
spill. I hold my liquor the same way
I hold conversation, the anticipation
of set up, punchline, the white milk
bathing the black outline. Subtext.
My heart, you have heard my language.

APHRODITE:

Yes, I was tomboyish –
climbing trees, scraping knees.
Yes, they put me in a dress. I remember
my school teacher bending over
my desk, teaching me alphabets. Now
I must speak –

Sweetheart, will you weave baskets
of nonce taxonomies so that I may
have a word for this hot, wet love?

air ii   /// *Christopher Kirubi/Dove*

sometimes on the street i pass
a wanderer   who swings
sweetshaped   as an apple
unfollowed fellow feeler
in a cloud of pocket music
the voices of those
in the past   dreaming of
thin papers   the rolling hills
of burgess park always

the gentle vibrations
cans in a plastic bag
loyal   to the slow pace
low life   let the breeze
keep the time   keep
       sleeping
dissolute accomplices
diffuse explanations
just a jaywalk away... . . ,

—,& what of the licked edge
of the work of dawdling
    ungrafted from
these doubts

of dreams
    unoccupied
the grid of
      insatiable

      accelerating

      animate depths

, breath   unsustainable
    swollen

      eye   & ear
       -ly errors

         ,—?
       ~~(life   !~~
       cannot be argued
       inflicted or alleviated
       a smoke   a

-fraid of its own
directness , the field
of its own
distortions
,—but i can
be punctuated
by fear   by f
-light,),

pattern
  & power   just
-ifications
in the frame
-work
&—!,(
) i—! unreal
-istic in
-sistent
insolent & in
-subordinate
#𝆑𝆑𝆑𝆑𝆑

-rustrate
-d   —!
. spec   -ulate
hope
-lessly late
-nt

, i know noose

noise

, no—!   (—&, on time

i know   very little)

o—!   , little time   keep

-ing this high

-ly activ

-ated   *k*

-otic

state

~~pro~~

con

-ductive

La Hora de las Brujas / Shamaness
/// *Antonela Pallini-Zemin*

Meet me a la hora de las brujas if you can't sleep
Enter my dream without asking permiso, no te vas a arrepentir
But there's something de lo que te tengo que advertir
Once you wake up, you'll find love no more in anyone else
You see, when you've peeped into the dreams of an awaken self
Ves todo como debería ser, ves the tall trees dancing with their
Twelve hundred feet, a witch's tongue the length of the Amazonas,
God's dark eye and bright eye todo el día, al mismo tiempo, 24/7,
The purple water in an endless creek, a woman on both borders
Doubling herself in flesh and speech, the repetition of the beat
Of a waterpecker blowing bubbles in the bottom of the creek,
La presencia de la Pachamama and the absence of la luz mala,
You see the seven hooves of a horse inhaling the earth
Propelling him or her to the air, you smell the untamed rain
And its rightful rhythm going astray, you hear the zigzag hissing
Of the wavy movement of the torso of the shamaness you've come
To visit and learn, you cup her inviting heart and feel your palma
Sweat the tears of your past, como los gatos she transmutes wounds
Mientras duerme, so no te preocupes that she'll be alright,
But you won't be able to turn around, she will hold you for a minute
Too long, longer than your social distance, but enough for her
Para hacerte apreciar que hay una diferencia entre 'me gustás' y
'Me encantás', y es que las curanderas encantan, specially when they
Are crabs, earthly dragons, angel hearts, rabbit fur, owl eyes,

There's a world of abrazos, de lazos de amor, en los arms de
Las mujeres de la tierra, soft lips, grounding bites, refrains of love,
Amor en su forma mejor, expressed outloud; so think twice
Before you decide to visit me at witches' time, porque después
De hacerlo, there'll be no way back to mundane arms.

An Ordered List of Barriers to Queer Intimacy [extracts]   /// *jack/lilidh*

WHAT'S GOTTEN IN THE WAY RECENTLY? (1)

1. Hair,   long or short.
2. Nails,   short or long.
3. Bra clasps.
4. A blindness to signs. (And who told you the chase could never be queer?)
5. A particularly misplaced piercing. (Seba! You begged me to pierce you—)
6. Doc Martens and their impenetrable laces! One day I'll figure out how to take off trousers without taking off shoes, one day I'll figure
7. Turtlenecks.
    a) and
8. Dungarees. One day I'll figure how to love you, without 1000 seminal lovers
    a) One day I'll figure being without reference to the other!
    b) One day I'll pull myself up by my doc marten laces! I'll no be indebted to any of youse
9. I'll kiss 1000 seminal tongues

10. And one day, I will pay my debts to 1000 seminal lovers
   a) Every having been raised by every other

BARRIERS TO QUEER INTIMACY (3)

16. I was using the English spelling of my name, when we met. Have you forgotten what they said about us in those plasticine halls?

17. Having straight flatmates.

    a) The comparative volume levels of Love Island omnibus and the G.L.O.S.S. playlist I have on to drown out the Love Island are not a matter for discussion, Kathrine. They are the site of contemporary queer praxis.

18. Having gay flatmates.

    a) One day I'll tire of watching it all play out: you and her in the kitchen with that cadence of lovers. You dance when you don't touch, too. I'm sure she's nice, but I don't need to overhear But I'm A Cheerleader again. I just need to get a spoon for my— Oh you made lasagna together? And biscuits? That's so— Oh no I've got my— well I'll maybe have a biscuit

    b) At least with straights fuck quicker, god

19. Do parents tire? You'll remember and you'll feel like an intruder. You'll make a half-joke, between kisses, and try to laugh:—your very own barrier

five years ago I was using the english spelling of my name I will love you I will love you until you raise yourself in secret I will raise you I will love you and I will raise you we will raise each-other and I will try to raise you first

[SEX AND HARM] (4)

20. do you feel safe? if i turn the big light off and the fairy lights on? lets have tea first, maybe, i'll make a pot, and we can sit on the bed, and you can tell me what you're feeling

    a) i don't do this much often either

    b) lowercase-i don't do much at all

21. When's the last time you had sex sober?

22. What do you need to disassociate from?

23. Unsafe sex (ph.) / ʌnˈseɪf sɛks/

    a) Sex which risks the transfer of STIs.

    b) Sex in which you are unsafe.

        i. Sex with people who don't value you.

        ii. Sex and its care which does not value your wellbeing.

        iii. Using kink to perform a role, rather than exist yourself.

        iv. Using kink to disassociate.

    c) Sex in which you will make your wellbeing unsafe.

        i. I had tried very hard, a long time ago. It was the trying that was wrong.

            [ ]

            [ ]

Cearcall-Suidhe   /// *Christopher Whyte*

Is mi nam phàiste, b' ann dìreach às dèidh
mo mhàthar a bu mhiann leam an taigh-beag
ùisneachadh, bhon a bhiodh an cearcall-suidhe
fhathast a' gleidheadh teas a colna fhèin,

's mise ga fhaireachdainn le mo mhàs rùisgte.
Cha bhrathainn riamh facal mun àbhaisteachd
ri neach sam bith. B' e giùlan coirbt' a bh' ann,
math dh'fhaodte, 's mi 'g innleachadh seòil neo-dhìrich

air faisge nach tairgte an gnìomhtharra
gach latha fhaotainn, a bha mi ag iarraidh.
Bidh pailteas smaointeannan is plòighean coirbte,
breisleachail foillsichte leis a' chloinn.

Bha i daonnan a' smocadh. Chomharraich
a làthaireachd am measgadh eadar boladh
an tombaca 's cùbhraidheachd a chleachd i,
's gainne cionacrachaidh am beath' a' phàist' ud.

Toilet Seat /// *Christopher Whyte*

When I was a child, I loved to use
the toilet immediately after my mother
because the oval seat on top of it
still conserved some of her body's warmth,

which I could enjoy with my bare backside.
I never spoke a word about the habit
to anyone. Maybe my behaviour
was twisted, working out this indirect

way of enjoying a closeness everyday
life had no place for, something which I lacked.
Children come up with all sorts of perverted
thoughts and fantastical contrivances.

She never stopped smoking. Her presence was marked
by a combination of tobacco
and the perfume she preferred to use.
There were not many caresses in that child's life.

Eulogy for a Young Sailor /// *Jay Gao*

I longed to terraform a hydraulic   empire,
silent nation with state of the art   oceans,
waterscapes, both natural and   speculative
catastrophes. Wet ports with no decks   to
smuggle your vesselled cargo or   possessions
overseas, your ancient customs. How   can
I cruise a non-native body in the body   of
a ship? In the margins of a galley: an   epic's
wreck. My borderless mission was   always
to rest, to slow time down a little,   descend
a little, wait a little differently, mourn   a
little more, to sink that sun, lose this   war,
return to our bloated coast a little,   become
a little too modern; so that I could   learn
to flow, to love, to curse, to fill out   these
splendid censuses, whisper irrigated   verse
to extinct birds and other classical   denizens,
to circle back and bury any loosened   foot-
notes in the sand with the most tender   of
contracts marked onto fraternity   paddles.
In a hundred years I might return to   find
your eyes chewed through by new   regimes
of invading worker ants dreaming of   one
precarious word to free them from   their
homely duties. I celebrated your tan,   your
smile, your green willingness to wage   hot
war. So when my late tribute came out   as

wordless as the long indelible line   refusing
erasure, each countersentence formed   scars
swimming across the sea's skin. I admit   our
midnight territories did seem as   everlasting
as traces of the mythic invisible ink we   tried
to ship, as dim as the soft inside curve   from
a blue shield shared, broken, bent way out   of
its form, disoriented, still raised high after   we

The River Turns into a Waterfall
/// *Andrés N. Ordorica*

the beavers
are making den
on the edge
where the river

      turns

      into

      a waterfall

      at the place

      their den

      becomes

      a dam

a beaver den (or lodge)
is a seasonal home
entered through water

           free from predators

           tucked away neatly

           hidden in the forest

      i am a beaver

         edging his way

            toward

            the lodge

under murky water
tall-yellowed reeds
      cattails swaying
      i find them

my fellow beavers
      they ask me

              will you help today
              will you make den
              with us?

aye my friends
today
i will make a den
to pass the winter in

and when
spring comes
           i will swim back
           to the surface
        breathe in
        the flowery air
        renewed and free

Under God's Eye
/// *Courtney Conrad*

I recite the full scripture,
while his fingers drill under
the open bible across my lap.
His trousers bulge,
the choir stifles my protest,
fingernails carving pew.
There are many girls.
Braids mushing into the gravel,
foetal crouches under staircases.
Collection plates brim with tears.
My testimony, a commotion.
Elders say *you have forgiven*
a liar and a thief.
Why harp on his misdirection?
He is not a murderer.
I want a crucifixion,
his penis to become a pillar of salt.
At the altar, I repent
for his trespasses against me.
I do not request forgiveness
for the kiss from my best friend.
She waits for the elders to march
out like the Israelites; before
rosary bead rubs birth spiritual shakes.
Stained-glass and musty seat cushions,
God's mansion is a trap house.

Museum of Survival; exhibit s.1516891
/// *Helen Bowie*

Date(s): 05-08-2011

Container: Desk draw III, 11f1 StRoEH9

Scope and Contents: Blister pack 'Temazepam'; Prescription bottle 'Quetiapine'; Postcard; Sachet Lubricant; Lipstick

Notes: Blister pack empty, crushed, as if opened hurriedly; Prescription bottle almost full, medication not taken; Postcard reads 'Put your crash helmet on, you're going through the headboard', reverse side blank except for one telephone number; lubricant bears sticker reading 'FURBURGER WEDNESDAYS'; lipstick cap missing, dark red wax exposed, colour 'Dare'

Object wall plaque: The artist presents a drawer. Two medications; two sides; duality and discovery; mania and magic; take one, leave one; leave it, not worth it; leave me alone, leave me alone, leave me alone. A postcard; a flirtation; a warning; an invitation; a red flag; a phone line; disconnected; dead lines; dead ends; dead. Lubricated evenings; no more friction; given the slip; going down, down, down; an easy in, an easy out. Lost lipstick caps; innards opened; the softness unprotected; crushed; trailing red; the last kiss parted from lips; now only stains. A drawer; a vessel; a memory; exposed.

ghazal: a sign from Allah /// *Deenah Al-Aqsa*

relax, recline, love,
i promise deenah's got you,

we sit, contemplate, try to define love,
talk endlessly into the night

you so often question the divine, love,
yet in the same breath you say 'i'll pray for you'

and mean it - your faith is no less sublime, love,
if it's not in the heavens above. no, somehow,

your faith in me has never weathered with time, love,
nor with strife or pain or loss,

nor with your good days and bad, nor mine, love -
my faith in the almighty wavers, but yours,

in the sheer, defiant belief that i can be kind, love,
a beacon of shimmering light reflected on oceans

my north star when i begged the Lord for a sign, love,
something, anything to make life worth living

sometimes, i think of your eyes, how they shine, love,
your hair, morning-mussed, auburn in the sun

more than sometimes, i imagine our fingers entwined, love,
i think of your hands, of your smile, tongue between teeth –

i think of a world in which i had a drop more steel in my spine, love,
a universe where the strongest steel was forged in your heart's fire,

where you and i were happy in this made-up world of mine, love,
where i could kiss you with abandon, walk with you arm-in-arm,

in reality - waiting, wishing, wanting things to align, love –
i yearn in silence, stay quiet, keep my feelings to my chest,

so only in my dreams will i tell you - lie back, supine, love,
let me love you here, in this perfect world of mine, love.

the Long Mynd   /// *Jack Bigglestone*

forever the always horizon sings receding
in nearly breaking falsetto
set to the edge
of the marked note
but holds back against the ear trick
the easy harmony
pulls silver along rosined strings
but not quite unbuckled to run
I'm forever walking
up half-remembered hills
till the brink rolls beyond
and I catch a signal
so send rose gifs as reply to all
hoping they will watch petals unfold endless
but shimmer and blooming
is its weary expense

there is a shepherd's whistle tone rising
and still rising

say we must imagine Sisyphus happy
have you never imagined him tired?
turning away

Norway /// *Kat Dixon*

you're on a boat with a woman you're supposed to love
trees grow out of the mountain   waterfalls are high huge
strong   the boat draws close so that you   the woman
you're supposed to love   the strangers you are sharing
this experience with   can reach out   fill a glass of water
you take photos   you reach over the side   fill a glass of
water   out here it's impossible to ignore   flecks of water
on the camera lens   you drink the water   exclaim how
fresh it tastes   you've never tasted water so fresh   her
body is facing towards the mountains   her body is facing
away from you   the water is really very fresh   Debbie
from Canada says she won't be able to drink the water back
home   now she's tasted this   the glasses aren't glasses
they are made from single use plastic   for all the people
who did this before   for all the people who will do this
after you   a man gets the zip caught on his mac   his
wife helps him   she is a barrister from Maine   when
is your lover not your lover   the engines are loud against
the mountains   if the mountains could shake they would
shake

Mellishon   /// *Harry Josephine Giles*

t o 5 m g	Here is my prayer:	glides over sea or back and forth alo
1 2 0	that you will die	do not pass it on to others. It may har
t o 2 0 m g	after a long & happy life	note that individual variation
0	& when you ascend & pass	if your symptoms seriously
t o 2 m g	through the gates & greet	single birds often fly low ove
3	the recording angel & ask	you are at an increased risk
. 2 5 g	"Was I right? Was it	somewhat more elastic and fast w
0	right, what I did?",	ask you about your own and your f
t o 4 g	your face still pinned by shame,	communally in winter
2	she will say, "What?	the benefits and risks of continuir
o m c g	Oh, well... let's check..."	usually alternates between a q
4 9	& lead you to the Hall of Lives	if you are not sure abou
. 0 5 m g	explaining with gentle hesitance	highly vocal, often he
2	that records without consequence	stop using it at onc
5 t o 2 m g	are only kept for five years before	occasionally so stror
6 9 0	dissolution into the stuff of being,	a history of excessiv
t o 2 m g	& that after half an hour of searching	plain, very pale
5	& checking her watch she will say,	if you still have you
t o 2 0 m g	"I'm sorry, I'm afraid my shift's over,	rather plain head
7 8	but feel free to stay.	you will have a bleed once a mont
t o 2 m g	I'm sure you're here somewhere."	upperparts and und
5	& that will you look up	important that you inform the
t o 2 0 m g	at the not-quite-infinite	unmistakeable in flight: broa
3 0	-but-always-expanding	and if one travels to the lungs
t o 2 m g	stacks of meaning,	a shallow depression, defended wi
2	the tall rolling ladders,	will not prevent memory loss.
o m g	& never learn how to leave.	keeps watch from top of i

everyone is still alive.
/// *Joelle Taylor*

(1)

everyone
is still alive.

on the stage
a drag queen is peeling

down to the pith of a boy
who is stripping to the kernel of a first kiss

light bankrupts the bathroom
as a woman steps out of her wound

the drapes smacking their lips
behind her to the roar of closet doors

& the bar serves pints of belief
that drip down our pink gingham shirts

we Ben Sherman she men
we bull footed women;

a shoal of old bois in herringbone suits
pilot the bar, bioluminescent

brave as bank holidays
leading us to safer waters

a way out of the net.

& the dance floor
is a collapsed lung

a hole healed
in the chest of a boi

her smile a blue and white cordon
around a loud body.

(11)

at the back of the bar
a woman shaves her hair
down to a crystal ball.
in it we are building a city
of mirrors
we are learning to look at ourselves
we are building a city of ghosts
There
a man is stopped by a swarm of bright boys
& given small gifts of indifference
There
we unugly ourselves
There
it is impossible for a woman to dress as a man
There
clothes become clothes
you can only dress as yourself
There
violence is two men not kissing
There
they wonder at rainbows in shop windows
There
rainbows are not for sale
There
they are scars.

(III)

we are hasty skinned
bone humming

burying dead names beneath patios
we are coming

camouflaged as ourselves
we are coming

in chorus lines of silence
bruised suits with lightning linings
we are coming

the tattoo of an anchor on a wrist
breadcrumbs of handkerchiefs
stepping away from our shadows
dressed as our fathers
dressed as absence
we are coming

the boy who gives birth to a girl
the girl who gives birth to herself

all the Gaultier grins
all the brogues & Harringtons
Levis & doc martins
a bouquet of cocked green carnations

we are coming.

(**iv**)

bless the myth of us
bless the mess of us
bless cliche and chaos
our untidy hearts

& the bar raises a pint to my people
my bois my butches
my queens queers & faggots
& for a moment
our faces are held there
preserved in the amber of lager

& everything is possible
everyone is still alive

rising to the surface

(in case of emergency
break

        glass).

/// *Commissioned by Edinburgh International Festival 2021* ///

About the Poets

Mary Jean Chan is the author of *Flèche*, published by
Faber & Faber (2019) and Faber USA (2020). *Flèche* won
the 2019 Costa Book Award for Poetry and was shortlisted
in 2020 for the International Dylan Thomas Prize, the
John Pollard Foundation International Poetry Prize,
the Jhalak Prize and the Seamus Heaney Centre First
Collection Poetry Prize. In 2021, *Flèche* was a Lambda
Literary Award Finalist. Chan won the 2018 Geoffrey
Dearmer Prize and was shortlisted for the Forward Prize
for Best Single Poem twice, receiving an Eric Gregory
Award in 2019. In Spring 2020, Chan was guest co-editor
alongside Will Harris at *The Poetry Review*. Chan is Senior
Lecturer in Creative Writing (Poetry) at Oxford Brookes
University. Born and raised in Hong Kong, they currently
live in Oxford.

Harry Josephine Giles is a writer and performer from
Orkney, living in Leith. Their verse novel *Deep Wheel
Orcadia* was published by Picador in October 2021. Their
poetry collections *The Games* (Out-Spoken Press, 2018)
and *Tonguit* (Freight Books 2015) were between them
shortlisted for the Forward Prize for Best First Collection,
the Saltire Prize and the Edwin Morgan Poetry Award.
They have a PhD in Creative Writing from the University
of Stirling. Their show Drone debuted in the Made in
Scotland Showcase at the 2019 Edinburgh Fringe and
toured internationally, and their performance *What We
Owe* was picked by the Guardian's best-of-the-Fringe 2013

roundup – in the "But Is It Art?" category.
www.harryjosephine.com

Andrew McMillan's first collection, *physical*, was the
first poetry collection to win the Guardian First Book
Award; it also won a Somerset Maugham Award, an Eric
Gregory Award, a Northern Writers' Award and the
Aldeburgh First Collection Prize. In 2019 it was voted as
one of the top 25 poetry books of the past 25 years by the
Booksellers Association. His second collection, *playtime,*
won the inaugural Polari Prize. He is a senior lecturer at the
Manchester Writing School at Manchester Metropolitan
University and is a fellow of the Royal Society of Literature.
His third collection is *pandemonium* (2021, Jonathan Cape).

Nat Raha is a poet and queer/trans activist-scholar, based
in Edinburgh. She is the author of three collections of poetry
including *of sirens, body & faultlines* (Boiler House Press,
2018), *countersonnets* (Contraband Books, 2013) and *Octet*
(Veer Books, 2010). Her creative and critical writing has
appeared in South Atlantic Quarterly, Poetry Review, MAP
Magazine, The New Feminist Literary Studies (Cambridge
UP, 2020), and Transgender Marxism (Pluto Press, 2021).
With Fiona Anderson and Glyn Davis, she co-edited
'Imagining Queer Europe Then and Now', a special issue of
Third Text journal (January 2021). Nat is a Research Fellow
on the 'Life Support: Forms of Care in Art and Activism'
project at the University of St Andrews, which will open an
exhibition at Glasgow Women's Library in August 2021. She
co-edits Radical Transfeminism Zine.

Christopher Whyte has so far published 7 collections of poems in Scottish Gaelic, most recently *Ceum air cheum / Step By Step* (2019) and *Leanabachd a' Cho-Ghleusaiche* (2020). He is the author of four novels in English, which include *The Warlock of Strathearn* (1997) and *The Gay Decameron* (1998) and has also translated five books of the poet Marina Tsvetaeva's work from Russian into English. Last to appear was *Youthful Verses* (2020). He abandoned a distinguished academic career to write full time in 2005 and since then has been based in Budapest, Hungary. www.christopherwhyte.com

Joelle Taylor is an award-winning poet and author who prior to the pandemic completed a world tour with her collection *Songs My Enemy Taught Me.* She founded SLAMbassadors, the UK national youth poetry slam championships, as well as the international spoken-word project Borderlines. She is widely anthologised, the author of 4 collections of poetry and is currently completing her debut collection of inter-connecting short stories *The Night Alphabet.* Her new book *C+NTO & Othered Poems* was published in June 2021 and is the subject of the Radio 4 arts documentary 'Butch'. *C+nto* has been named by The Telegraph as one of the books of the year, as well as DIVA magazine's Book of the Month, and awarded 5 stars by the Morning Star. It has also been awarded the TS Eliot Prize 2021. She has received a Changemaker Award from the Southbank Centre; a Fellowship of the RSA; and her poem 'Valentine' was Highly Commended in the Forward Prize. She is a co-curator and host of Out-Spoken Live, a poetry and music club currently resident at the Southbank Centre; and the commissioning editor at Out-Spoken Press.

Renowned for her performances on page and stage, **Patience Agbabi's** poems have been broadcast on television and radio all over the world. Her work has also appeared on the London Underground and human skin. In 2004 she was nominated one of the UK's Next Generation Poets, and in 2017 she was elected as a Fellow of the Royal Society of Literature. She has lectured in Creative Writing at several UK universities including Greenwich, Cardiff and Kent. She's published 4 poetry collections, *R.A.W.* (Gecko Press, 1995), *Transformatrix* (Canongate Books, 2000), *Bloodshot Monochrome* (Canongate, 2008), and *Telling Tales* (Canongate, 2014), which was shortlisted for the Ted Hughes Award. In 2018, she was writer-in-residence at the Brontë Parsonage Museum. She is currently a Fellow in Creative Writing at Oxford Brookes University.

Dean Atta is a British author hailing from London and living in Glasgow. He is a member of Malika's Poetry Kitchen and a patron of LGBT+ History Month. His young-adult novel in verse, *The Black Flamingo*, won the 2020 Stonewall Book Award and was shortlisted for the CILIP Carnegie Medal, Jhalak Prize, Los Angeles Times Book Prize and Waterstones Children's Book Prize. 2022 sees the publication of his second young-adult novel in verse, *Only on the Weekends*, as well as his second poetry collection, *There is (still) love here*.

Jay Gao is the author of *Imperium* (2022), forthcoming from Carcanet Press, as well as three poetry pamphlets. He is a Contributing Editor for *The White Review*, and is studying for an MFA at Brown University.

Helen Bowie (they/she) is a poet, performer and charity worker based in Glasgow. They are the author of two poetry pamphlets, *WORD/PLAY* (Beir Bua Press, 2021) and *Exposition Ladies* (Fly on the Wall Press, 2022). She is extremely online at @helensulis.

Jack Cooper is a science communicator living in London. His poetry has featured in publications such as Ambit, Popshot, and Young Poets Network, and was recently discussed on BBC Radio 4. The Poetry Society resource "We Are Cellular" uses his poetry to teach senior school students about metaphor and biology.

Sam J Grudgings is a queer poet from Bristol shortlisted for the Outspoken Poetry Prize 2020. His work explores rehabilitation, addiction & loss via the lens of body horror & the 1920's burlesque scene. Commonly found yelling poems at punk shows, his collection *The Bible II* is available from Verve Poetry Press.

Andrés N. Ordorica is a queer Latinx writer based in Edinburgh. His writing attempts to map the journey of his diasporic experience and unpack what it means to be from ni de aquí, ni de allá. His debut poetry collection, *At Least This I Know,* is published with 404 Ink.

Kira Scott is a writer, bookseller and English Literature graduate from East Lothian. Her work was published in The Common Breath's *The Middle of a Sentence* and she was shortlisted for the Writers & Artists Working-Class Writers' Prize 2021. www.kirascott.co.uk

Oluwaseun Olayiwola is a Nigerian-American dancer, choreographer, poet, and critic based in London. He recently completed an MFA in Choreography from the Trinity Laban Conservatoire of Music in Dance. His poems have been published by the Tate, bath magg, Odd Magazine, Queerlings, VS the Podcast and Poached Hare.

Deenah Al-Aqsa is an activist and award-nominated journalist. As a queer Muslim woman, she wants to explore every facet of her heritage and faith through writing, staying true to the defiant Bengali rebellion that runs through her blood. She loves tea, cats and comics, in that order.

JP Seabright (she/they) is a queer writer living in London. They have three pamphlets published: *Fragments from Before the Fall: An Anthology in Post-Anthropocene Poetry* by Beir Bua Press; the erotic memoir *NO HOLDS BARRED* by Lupercalia Press, and *GenderFux,* a collaborative poetry pamphlet, by Nine Pens Press.

Mariam Marsimashvili is a bilingual poet recently graduated from Goldsmiths University where she studied literature and creative writing. She lives in Oxford and is inspired by all things strange. Someday, she wants to be the David Lynch of the poetry world. You can find more of her poems on her website. linktr.ee/mariamvars

Jack Bigglestone is a writer and reader from rural Shropshire, he now lives in Scotland. With a surname like that you can easily find him and more of his work online.

Kat Payne Ware (she/her) is a queer poet and essayist, and the founding editor of *SPOONFEED*, an online literary food magazine. Her debut pamphlet of poetry, *THE LIVE ALBUM*, was published with Broken Sleep Books in July 2021. You can find her on Twitter @katpayneware and @SPOONFEEDmag.

Lady Red Ego is a lesbian writer concerned with intimacies. Her first pamphlet, *The Red Ego,* was published in 2019 with Wild Pressed Books and her second pamphlet, *Natural Sugars,* was published in 2020 by Broken Sleep Books. You can find her at: www.ladyredego.com

jack / lilidh: An Aberdonian graduate, Jack is a Glasgow-based writer and performer. She lived for several years as a recluse in Aberdeenshire. Is still slightly unhinged. Some of her writing is for sale on etsy, and some news-writing available online; under 'jack/lilidh,' or 'Lilidh Jack.' Updates at @jacklilidh.

Antonela Pallini-Zemin writes both in English and Spanish and is currently doing a postgraduate Specialisation in Literary Translation. She holds an MA in Creative Writing by UEA. Her poems have been published in different newspapers, literary magazines and journals across the UK, the US, Mexico, Argentina, and Spain. Twitter: @PalliniZemin

Jinhao Xie, born in Chengdu, is interested in nature, the mundane, the interpersonal and selfhood. A Barbican Young Poet and a member of Southbank Centre New Poets Collective. Their work is in POETRY, Gutter Magazine, Poetry Review, Harana, Bath Magg, and elsewhere. You can find them @xie.jin.hao (Instagram), @jinisnotfound (Twitter)

Kat Dixon (she/her) is a queer, London-based poet. Her poems have appeared in The Rialto, Perverse, Butcher's Dog, Queerlings, South Bank Poetry and Mslexia. She recently graduated from an MA in Writing Poetry with Newcastle University and The Poetry School. @dixon_kat (Instagram) @katdixon2012 (Twitter)

Courtney Conrad is a Jamaican poet. A member of The London Library Emerging Writers Programme and a Barbican Young Poets. A Bridport Prize Young Writers Award recipient shortlisted for The White Review Poet's Prize and Oxford Brookes International Poetry Competition and longlisted for the Rebecca Swift Women Poets' Prize.

Mae Diansangu is an Aberdonian poet. Mae writes to continue conversations started by people long gone and some who are still here. These conversations are felt in the body before being expressed on the page, making each poem a visceral response (to a question that will probably remain unanswered).

Christopher Kirubi/Dove is a London based artist and poet.

Mina C is a poet and student from London.

* * *

Co-ditor **Éadaoín Lynch** is an Irish poet & researcher based in Edinburgh, whose work has been published previously in The Kindling Journal, the Fawn Press anthology Elements, and shortlisted for the Jane Martin Poetry Prize and the London Magazine Poetry Prize. Their debut pamphlet, *Fierce Scrow*, is forthcoming from Nine Pens Press in August 2022.

Co-editor **Alycia Pirmohamed** is author of the pamphlets *Hinge* and *Faces that Fled the Wind*, and co-author of *Second Memory*. In 2020 Alycia was the winner of the Edwin Morgan Poetry Award. Her debut poetry collection *Another Way to Split Water* is forthcoming with YesYes Books (US) and Polygon Books (UK) in 2022.

STEWED RHUBARB